Livonia Public Library
ALFRED NOBLE BRANCH
32901 PLYMOUTH ROAD
Livonia, Michigan 48150
421-6600

J
592
5

Settel, Joanne.
  How do ants know when you're having a
picnic : and other questions kids ask about
insects and other crawly things / by Joanne
Settel, Nancy Baggett ; illustrated by Linda
Tunney. -- New York : Atheneum, 1986.

  92 p. : ill. ; slj 4-7   82874

  SUMMARY: Answers questions about insect and
other animal behavior, such as "Why do
earthworms come out in the rain?"
  ISBN 0-689-31268-7: $11.95   AUG 8 7

  1. Invertebrates. 2. Insects.   I.
Baggett, Nancy. II. Title.

QL364.2.S38 198

Books by Joanne Settel and Nancy Baggett

Why Does My Nose Run?
And Other Questions Kids Ask About Their Bodies

How Do Ants Know When You're Having a Picnic?

HOW
DO ANTS KNOW
WHEN YOU'RE
HAVING A
PICNIC
?

HOW
DO ANTS KNOW
WHEN YOU'RE
HAVING A
PICNIC
?

(AND OTHER QUESTIONS KIDS ASK
ABOUT INSECTS AND OTHER
CRAWLY THINGS)

JOANNE SETTEL
NANCY BAGGETT
ILLUSTRATED BY LINDA TUNNEY

ATHENEUM / 1986 / NEW YORK

Text copyright © 1986 by Joanne Settel and Nancy Baggett
Illustrations copyright © 1986 by Linda Tunney

Atheneum
Macmillan Publishing Company
866 Third Avenue, New York, NY 10022

Text set by Fisher Composition, New York City
Printed & bound by Fairfield Graphics, Fairfield, Pennsylvania
Designed by Scott Chelius
First Edition

10 9 8 7 6 5 4 3 2 1

Library of Congress Cataloging in Publication Data

Settel, Joanne.
How do ants know when you're having a picnic?

SUMMARY: Answers questions about insect and other animal
behavior, such as "Why do earthworms come out in the rain?"
1. Invertebrates—Behavior—Miscellanea—Juvenile literature.
2. Insects—Behavior—Miscellanea—Juvenile literature.
[1. Invertebrates. 2. Insects. 3. Questions and answers]
I. Baggett, Nancy   II. Title
QL364.2.S38   1986   592   86-3353
ISBN 0-689-31268-7

OCT 19 1987

CONTENTS

HOW
DO ANTS KNOW
WHEN YOU'RE
HAVING A
PICNIC
?

INTRODUCTION

ABOUT INSECTS, BUGS AND OTHER CREEPY CRAWLY THINGS

This book is about some of the most interesting creatures in the world of nature. You may be used to calling them insects. Or perhaps you just refer to them as "bugs." The fact is, though, there's no one word that really describes all the "creepy crawlers" included here. Scientifically speaking, some are bugs, some are insects, and still others are "non-insects" of various kinds. Here are a few facts to help you straighten it all out.

To start with, a bug is an insect but an insect is not necessarily a bug! This may sound like a riddle to most people but to entomologists, or scientists who study insects, it is very simple.

When entomologists talk about "true bugs," they mean one particular group of insects. This category includes a lot of "buggy looking" creatures such as bedbugs (see page 51), stinkbugs, and squash bugs. It also includes an insect called the water strider, which looks more like a spider than a bug (see page 40).

Scientists have divided insects into a number of other different groups. For example, butterflies and moths are in one category, beetles in another, and bees, wasps, and ants in a third. As the chart on page 5 shows you, there are also groups for termites, fleas, flies, lice, and more.

In assigning creatures to groups, scientists study to see which ones have the same long-ago ancestors. They also consider how each species lives and what it looks like. The idea is to place similar insects together and the whole organizing process is known as *classification.*

In the course of this studying and classifying, experts have found that there are some creatures that seem similar to insects but don't quite belong in this group. For example, all species classified as insects have six legs. Since spiders and ticks each have eight legs, and millipedes and centipedes have many more than that, these species must fall into the "non-insect" category. In addition to these creepy crawlers, there are many others, such as the legless earthworms, leeches, and slugs, which are different enough from insects to each need a separate place on the classification chart.

CLASSIFICATION CHART
INVERTEBRATES
(ANIMALS WITHOUT BACKBONES)

Phylum: ARTHROPODS Crabs, Lobsters, Insects, Millipedes, Centipedes, Spiders, Mites, etc.

Class: INSECTS Bees, Butterflies, Beetles, Flies, Ants, Termites, etc.

Order: Odonata—Dragonflies

Order: Orthoptera—Grasshoppers, Crickets, Seventeen Year Locusts (Periodic Cicadas)

Order: Isoptera—Termites

Order: Anoplura—Sucking Lice

Order: Lepidoptera—Butterflies, Moths, Inchworms (Moth Larvae), Tent Caterpillars (Moth Larvae), Silkworms (Moth Larvae)

Order: Dictyoptera—Cockroaches, Praying Mantises

Order: Hemiptera (True Bugs)—Bedbugs, Water Striders

Order: Coleoptera—Japanese Beetles, Fireflies, Ladybugs

Order: Diptera—Flies, Mosquitoes

Order: Siphonaptera—Fleas

Order: Hymenoptera—Bees, Wasps, Ants

Class: ARACHNIDS—Spiders, Scorpions, Mites, etc.

Order: Araneida—Spiders, Tarantulas

Order: Opiliones—Daddy Longlegs (Harvestmen)

Order: Acarina—Ticks

Class: DIPLOPODS—Millipedes

Class: CHILOPODS—Centipedes

Phylum: ANNELIDS—Clam worms, Earthworms, Marine worms, etc.

Class: OLIGOCHAETA—Earthworms

Class: HIRUDINEA—Leeches

Phylum: MOLLUSKS—Squids, Oysters, Clams, Snails, etc.

Class: GASTROPODS—Snails, Slugs

Phylum: PLATYHELMINTHES—Flukes, Flatworms, Tapeworms

Class: Cestoda—Tapeworms

WHY ARE THERE SO MANY INSECTS?

A female fruit fly can lay 3,000 eggs during the one month of her adult life. Each of those eggs may produce a mature adult fruit fly in a matter of weeks. These new adults in turn produce more eggs. If half of the first 3,000 eggs develop into female fruit flies, and each of these lays 3,000 eggs, you'll have approximately 4,500,000 new eggs in less than three months!

Fruit flies are just one example of insects that lay huge numbers of eggs. A queen bee can lay more than 300,000 eggs during her lifetime. With insects producing so many offspring in such short periods of time, it is not surprising that there are vast numbers of insects in the world.

Why do insects need to lay so many eggs? One reason is that insects are not generally designed to survive a long time. Many live out their entire lives in less than a year. Because they have such a short life span, parent insects aren't generally around when their offspring emerge as larvae. Young insects, unprotected by adults, can easily become a tasty meal for larger predators. To insure that at least some of their offspring survive, insects have evolved with the ability to lay large numbers of eggs.

Another reason why insects reproduce in such large numbers is that insects are designed to be tiny. Small size provides many benefits to the insect. It means that the animal can squeeze itself into the little cracks and crevices found on the bodies of plants and other larger animals. Insects can thus make their homes in all kinds of protected places where nothing else can live and where predators have trouble reaching them.

Unfortunately, being tiny is also dangerous. If an insect isn't careful, there's a good chance that it will get squashed by something bigger than it is. Thus, once again, it's a good idea for insects to lay large numbers of eggs. In this way the chances are increased that some of the young will make it to adulthood.

DO INSECTS HAVE BLOOD?

A swatted fly never leaves a single drop of red blood behind. That's not because flies don't have blood, it's just that their blood isn't red like ours.

Flies and other insects have a special kind of blood called *hemolymph*. Most often it is colorless, though occasionally it contains chemicals which make it yellow or green. Only a few insects have hemolymph with the bright redness that is found in the blood of humans and other vertebrates.

An insect's hemolymph is not red because it lacks the chemical hemoglobin. Hemoglobin, which is abundant in human blood, is normally used to pick up molecules or tiny amounts of life-giving oxygen from our lungs and carry the molecules to all the cells of our body. When oxygen combines with hemoglobin it turns bright red, giving our blood its characteristic color. Insects use oxygen, but usually it isn't transported to their cells by their hemolymph. Thus, they don't need hemoglobin.

Hemolymph, like human blood, circulates around the insect's body carrying nutrients to cells and waste products away from them. However, while human blood moves in closed blood vessels, insect blood simply gushes through the creature's body in what is known as an "open circulatory system."

The power for moving blood through the "open circulatory system" comes from a single long blood vessel which runs down the insect's back. This blood vessel acts something like a heart. It pumps hemolymph toward the insect's head. As the hemolymph moves out the front end of the vessel, it enters the insect's body cavity. Here the nourishing fluid bathes the animal's organs and tissues. Next, the hemolymph seeps back into the large blood vessel through holes at its rear end. In this way blood circulates around the insect's body.

While the open circulatory system works well for insects, it is far too slow for humans. It can take as long as thirty minutes for hemolymph to make its way around an insect's tiny body. In humans, however, blood makes a complete circuit through the closed system of blood vessels in only three minutes.

DO INSECTS LIVE IN THE ARCTIC?

When it's freezing cold in Fairbanks, Alaska, the arctic carabid beetle is alive and well, nibbling at chunks of rotting wood. This beetle is one of a small number of insects that can not only survive an arctic winter, but can also remain active at temperatures below freezing (32 degrees Farenheit). Other insects that manage to live through cold winters can only do it if they are buried in a hole, and in a state of sleep or dormancy (see "Where Do Insects Go in the Winter?").

The insect's secret to surviving the cold is antifreeze! We use antifreeze in our cars, to keep our radiator water from freezing during the winter. Similarly, certain insects use antifreeze in their blood to keep it from freezing when the air gets cold.

Cold-tolerant insects manufacture their own special antifreeze, usually a substance called glycerol. Glycerol production begins as soon as the air temperature falls to a dangerous level. For the arctic carabid beetle the formation of glycerol begins at 32 degrees Farenheit. As winter temperatures continue to drop the beetle makes more and more of the protective fluid. Then, in the spring, when the air warms up, antifreeze production stops and glycerol can no longer be found in the tiny animal's body.

One important way glycerol protects an insect is by making its body water less "freezable." This is important because an insect is made up of large amounts of water. There's water in its blood and in all of its cells. Normally, this water will freeze at 32 degrees Farenheit. When water freezes, the little parts, or molecules, that make up the liquid, hook together to form the hard, solid material we call ice. Glycerol molecules, however, get in the way of the water molecules and keep them from locking and becoming ice crystals. With glycerol in its blood, the arctic carabid beetle will not freeze until it reaches 25 degrees Farenheit.

Even better, though, is the effect of glycerol on *supercooling*. An animal becomes supercooled when its body temperature drops below freezing and it isn't frozen! Glycerol enables the insect to supercool in the following way. When the air temperature drops very slowly, glycerol does an excellent job of holding the water molecules apart. Under these conditions, the insect will not freeze until the temperature drops to -5 degrees Farenheit! Thus the animal's body temperature has dropped below its normal freezing point without freezing. Supercooling does not work if temperatures drop too quickly because the rapidly changing water molecules are very difficult to hold apart.

All this may sound nifty, but it still doesn't completely protect the arctic carabid and other insects that live in really cold places. Temperatures often drop as low as -60 degrees Farenheit. inside the decaying tree stumps where the beetle spends the winter. At these frigid temperatures the insect does freeze. While freezing means death for most insects, the arctic carabid simply thaws out in the spring and goes on its way. Here again, glycerol is the life saver. The amazing chemical is also able to thaw ice crystals in the insect's blood to keep them from getting into and damaging the delicate cells that make up the animal's body.

WHERE DO INSECTS GO IN THE WINTER?

Everyone knows that you don't get bee stings or mosquito bites when the air turns cold. Insects seem to vanish every winter, but most of the pesky little creatures don't actually leave, they merely go into hiding.

Insects cannot usually live in extreme cold because they don't have any internal heating systems to keep them warm. Scientists consider animals that cannot warm themselves to be *poikilothermal*. Such animals are generally the same temperature as the air that surrounds them. If a poikilothermatic tissues get too cold they will stop functioning properly and the animal will die. To prevent this, many insects spend the winter in a warm place. Here, they enter a period of temporary sleep called *diapause*.

Diapause in insects is something like hibernation in mammals. The insect first finds itself a nice, secure little nook where temperatures won't drop too low. This might be deep underground, inside the trunk of a rotting tree or even in the middle of a sheet of ice! (See "Do Insects Live in the Arctic?"). Once the insect is buried, all of its body processes slow down. The dormant animal stops eating and growing and breathes at a very slow rate.

It is the shortening daylight hours of the autumn that normally causes insects to enter diapause. The creatures remain in their slowed-down state throughout the winter. Then, as the days begin to lengthen in the spring, the insects emerge from their sleeping quarters and become active again.

The cold weather itself is not the thing that tells most insects that it is time to slow down their bodies. Nor do warm temperatures tell the animals that it's time to reemerge from winter sleep. The reason for this is that air temperatures are not reliable signs of the changing seasons. An animal could be fooled by the occasional warm days that occur in winter and the cool days that pop up during the summer. A sudden warm spell in the middle of winter, for example, could send an animal out of dormancy too soon. This would cause the unfortunate creatures to freeze when the cold weather returned.

However, days always get shorter in the winter and become long again in the summer. By using day length as a timer, the insect is sure to never get fooled.

WHY DO BEES BUZZ?

Bees are the best buzzers in the insect world. Not only do they have a number of different buzzes in their repertoire, but they buzz for a wide variety of reasons.

You've probably already heard the buzzing of bees in flight. The sound is produced by the rapid rotation of their wings through the air. Honeybees also make a soft buzzing sound when they fan their wings. Wing fanning is the rather remarkable method the bees use to cool their hive. When the hive gets too warm, workers perch near the entrance and, by rotating their wings, act like a fan to bring in fresh air.

If you've ever made the mistake of getting too close to a bees' or hornets' nest, you know these creatures can produce another kind of buzz as well. This loud, angry-sounding tone is the way bees warn nest mates of trouble. (Of course, it also means *you're* in trouble!) Interestingly, bees don't have any ear parts and can't hear one another's warning. Instead, they pick up the buzzing messages by feeling the vibrations of the sounds with their legs and antennae.

Honeybees also buzz during a special activity known as dancing. There are several different patterns of movements, or dances, and the remarkable little insects use these to communicate to hive mates when they discover a new source of food. In the waggle dance, for example, a bee begins by wagging her body, moving straight ahead, and buzzing. The dancer doesn't produce this buzzing by rotating the wings, but by shaking, or vibrating, her powerful flight muscles. It's as if she is revving up her engine before taking off! As amazing as it seems, her actions tell other gatherers of pollen and nectar exactly where to find the food. (See "How Do Honeybees Find Their Way Back to the Hive?")

Perhaps the niftiest buzz of all is produced by some species of bumblebees during pollen gathering. In certain plants, including tomatoes, the blossoms droop over and the pollen is at the back of a long tube. To collect its powdery prize, a bumblebee hangs upside down on a bloom and buzzes vigorously with its flight muscles. The vibrations of the insect's muscles and body against the plant loosen the pollen from the back of the blossom, and the gravity causes it to fall down the tube to the waiting bee!

HOW DO BEES MAKE HONEY?

Bees manufacture a product no other creatures in the world can produce—the delicious, syrupy sweet known as honey. Honey is made from nectar collected from flowers and other blooming plants. This raw material must be carefully processed and handled before it becomes honey. Here's how bees make their marvelous food.

First, worker bees suck up nectar from flowers. Then they tuck it away in a part of their abdomen called the honey stomach. When the nectar-laden bees return to the hive, they regurgitate, or force up, the sweet watery liquid to their mouthparts. Now, bees waiting in the hive take in the droplets and carry them to the wax comb. Sometimes the bees pass the liquid back and forth a number of times. Scientists think that as they do this the bees add chemicals that help break down the sugars in the nectar.

During the next stage of honeymaking, most of the excess water is removed from the droplets. First, the drops are deposited in empty cells and left until some of the moisture evaporates and the liquid thickens. Bees assist the drying process by fanning the air with their wings. They also pick up drops and suck them in and out with their mouthparts. After the drops are handled for several days, they are returned to the comb cells to ripen.

Finally, when most of the water has evaporated from the drops, the thick and sticky mixture is ready for storage. The bees release wax from their own wax-making glands and use it to cover each cell with a beeswax seal. Surprising as it may seem, the delectable mixture inside is no longer highly-concentrated nectar. Somehow, during processing, it has become the sweet, syrupy product that humans and bears, as well as bees, love to eat.

HOW DO HONEYBEES FIND THEIR WAY BACK TO THE HIVE?

A good memory and a remarkable brain are the special tools that the honeybee uses to find its way home. The brain of this small insect is like a carefully designed computer. It takes in information, stores it, and then makes surprisingly complicated calculations. In fact, the honeybee's learning and computing skills are the most advanced in the insect world.

The honeybee starts to learn its way by taking a good look at the hive and surrounding area the first few times it goes off to gather food. It does this by flying out of the hive, turning back and circling around for a few seconds. This gives the bee time to fix the important details and landmarks in its brain. For several days, the careful insect also practices its homing skills by flying out only short distances, then returning to the hive again. Gradually, as it becomes familiar with the territory, it travels to flowers and other food sources that are farther and farther away.

Although just getting home again might seem like a big enough job for the little food gatherer, scientists have discovered that the honeybee is also learning some astronomy on its trips. The creature soon recognizes that the sun always moves along the same path and memorizes its position in the sky at any second of the day. The bee can do this because, unlike humans, it has a built-in clock that constantly tells it the time.

Once the bee has assembled all this information, it performs some pretty fantastic feats. First, it uses the sun as a compass to find its way back to flowers it has discovered. In other words, the bee "knows" where the sun will be at any given time. If it is before twelve noon, the sun will be rising in

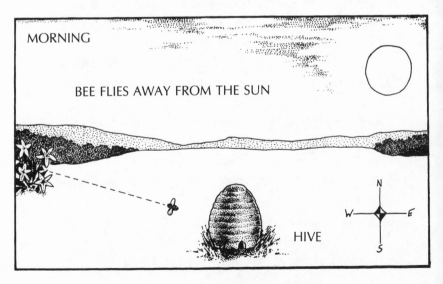

MORNING

BEE FLIES AWAY FROM THE SUN

HIVE

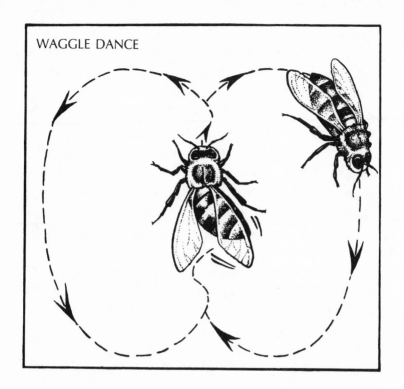

WAGGLE DANCE

the east. If it is after twelve noon, it will be sinking toward the west. The bee also remembers whether the flowers are located in the north, south, east, or west. Thus, the bee can check the position of the sun and tell which way it needs to fly to return to its feeding place. For example, if the sun is in the east and the flower is in the west, the bee knows it must fly directly away from the sun.

Perhaps even more amazing is the ability of the honeybee to "tell" other hive members where to find its nectar-filled flowers. The little traveler does this by performing a set of motions scientists call a dance, as we saw on page 13. During the pattern known as the waggle dance, the bee carefully chooses a position in the hive, wags its body, buzzes, and moves straight ahead. Then it stops wagging and buzzing and moves alternately to the right and left in a semicircle. Scientists have learned that this particular dance is the one used when the food source is far away. The dancer communicates the direction of the flowers by moving ahead at the same angle to the sun as it would when actually flying. It "tells" hive mates the distance to the feeding place by the speed of its dance. The farther away the food source is, the slower the dancer moves.

Without even trying, the bee furnishes one more clue. Its nest mates learn the kind of flower to look for just by noticing the odor of the pollen still clinging to the traveler's body.

ARE THERE REALLY "KILLER" BEES?

Yes, there are insects known as "killer" bees. They aren't big or scary-looking, but they have a very nasty disposition.

Actually, these insects, which scientists prefer to call "Brazilian" bees, are a new type of honeybee found in South America. They are the result of the accidental mating of a very aggressive bee imported from Africa with a honeybee common in Brazil. The resulting "killers" look a lot like the honeybees we have in the United States. And like our honeybees, these insects live in hives and are good honey and beeswax makers.

The problem with the Brazilian bees is their terrible temper. When their hive is disturbed they are much more likely than ordinary honeybees to swarm out and start stinging. They are also more likely to keep pursuing and attacking as their target flees. Researchers have demonstrated this by dangling a leather ball in front of different hives. When the ball is held a foot away and jiggled, it usually receives stings from two regular honeybees, but from about fourteen Brazilian bees! Also, ordinary honeybees usually chase the ball about seventy feet, while the Brazilian ones keep following and stinging for about five hundred feet! The Brazilian bees are so ill-tempered they have been known to attack and sting people and livestock until they died.

At this point, experts are still arguing about just how big a threat these little creatures really are to humans and farm animals. Researchers are also attempting to gradually improve the behavior of Brazilian bees by mating them with ordinary honeybees. Nobody knows yet how well this will work.

In addition, American experts worry about keeping these nasty creatures from spreading into our country. As scary as it sounds, some "killer" bees were recently discovered here, nesting in some oil drilling equipment on the California coast! Entomologists believe that the bees came along with the equipment when it was moved north from South America. The experts quickly got rid of the insects and carefully checked the surrounding territory to make sure they hadn't spread. The scientists say that although this particular threat is over, we'll have to stay alert so that no more Brazilian bees are brought in.

Nevertheless, the bees are gradually spreading and heading our way on their own! Will they really reach us? Will they still be ferocious? No one can say. The only good news is that "killer" bees are killed by cold winters, so they probably can't live in the northern part of the United States.

DO WASPS REALLY MAKE PAPER?

Not only do wasps make paper, but they have a complete paper-making kit right in their mouths! To begin making paper, the wasps use their mandibles, or mouthparts, and scrape bits of wood from an old fence, barn, or post. Then the industrious insects chew the wood, mixing it with their sticky saliva. The resulting paste can be stretched into thin strips of paper. These strips are used to build a tough yet lightweight nest.

Some familiar types of wasps that build paper nests are yellowjackets and hornets. Hornets are the most skilled, building giant, multileveled nests that they suspend from the branch of a tree or house eave.

Even the fanciest nests are started by a single wasp, the queen of the colony. The queen is the only member of the colony who manages to live through a cold winter. She buries herself in a hole in the ground and becomes dormant (see "Where Do Insects Go in the Winter?") until spring. When the weather warms, the queen emerges from the ground. Then she picks out a suitable spot, like a tree branch or an overhang on a house, where she can build her nest.

Using paper she produces herself, the queen makes an umbrella-shaped nest that is filled with small compartments. The whole umbrella hangs from a branch by a paper stem and is called a comb.

Once the basic nest is complete, the queen lays her eggs in the compartments of the comb. Soon the first brood of young wasps hatches out. The queen tends and feeds the newly hatched larvae until they mature into adult wasps. Then, they are ready to help the queen add new combs to the nest so she can lay more eggs. A completed hornet's nest can contain ten layers of combs all surrounded by a protective jacket of paper.

Now you might think that a nest made of paper would easily fall apart. Actually, though, paper made by wasps is quite strong. A hornet's nest will last long into the winter, even through wind, rain, and sleet.

Even more amazing is the paper that is made by certain species of wasps that live in tropical climates. These remarkable insects create paper that is so tough that the nests they build last for up to twenty years!

HOW DO FLIES WALK ON WALLS?

A fly doesn't use magic to walk up your wall, it uses six very special legs. At the end of each leg,

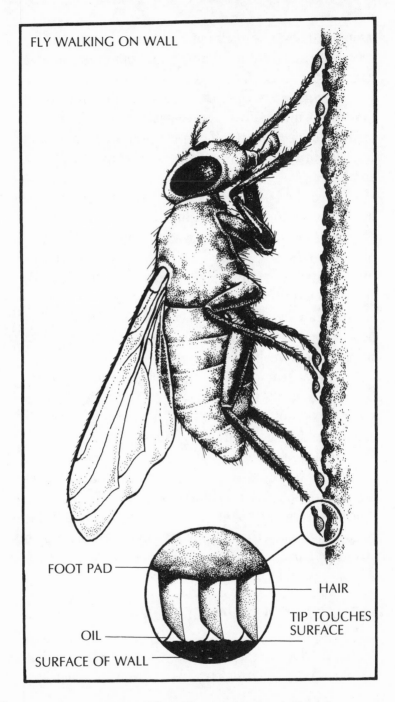

FLY WALKING ON WALL

FOOT PAD

HAIR

TIP TOUCHES SURFACE

OIL

SURFACE OF WALL

the fly has a pair of sharp claws and a soft, sticky pad. When the fly is climbing up, the claws enable it to cling to any tiny bumps or grooves in the wall's surface. Although the surface of your wall may look smooth to you, it's actually full of little cracks that give a fly a good "leg hold."

On smooth vertical surfaces like windowpanes, the fly's adhesive pads go into action. These soft pads are covered with very tiny hairs. The hairs are coated with oil. The hair ends angle upward like a sliding board. Only the pointy tip on the rear end of each hair touches the surface on which the fly walks. When the fly moves forward, the oil smooths the way. If, however, the hair is pushed backward, its tip presses down hard, breaking through the oil. This enables the hair to stick directly to the vertical surface, and keeps the fly from sliding backward. Thus, the fly can easily move its legs to walk up a windowpane and not slip back down with every step.

ARE FLIES REALLY DIRTY?

Any animal that feeds on dung and decaying plant and animal parts is bound to be dirty. Estimates are that a single fly carries a population of over two million bacteria on its tiny body! A fly that's made a recent visit to a pile of horse manure will carry whatever dirt it picks up to its next dining site. That may turn out to be your garbage can or even your dinner plate!

This does not mean that you should get upset every time a fly comes near. Not all bacteria are harmful to humans, and a few flies here and there are unlikely to carry enough harmful bacteria to cause any problems. However, in places where sanitation is poor and flies are everywhere, the little insects can become real problems as disease carriers. Houseflies are known to spread diseases such as dysentery and polio, as well as a variety of digestive tract ailments.

Houseflies, the most familiar of the 85,000 fly species, do not bite. Thus, they are only a problem to humans because they deposit bacteria in our homes and on the food we eat. Other related insects such as black flies, tse-tse flies, and mosquitoes bite humans and other animals to get their blood. These insects have become major human pests because they can deposit disease organisms directly into the bloodstream. Certain species are the cause of deadly diseases such as malaria and African sleeping sickness.

WHY DO FLIES WALK ALL OVER EVERYTHING?

The housefly uses its feet to eat! When this pesky insect wants to learn if something's edible, it simply steps on it. Amazing as it sounds, the housefly actually tastes with its feet. This unusual ability enables the animal to sense whether something is good to eat without having to suck it into its mouth.

The housefly begins its food sampling using the hundreds of tiny taste hairs that cover its feet. The hairs have special cells to detect sugar and salt. These taste cells are similar to the ones that humans have on their tongues. Unlike humans, however, flies also have cells that detect water (humans can taste the sweetness, saltiness, sourness, or bitterness of substances dissolved in water, but not water itself).

Only if the fly's sensitive feet send the insect's brain the message "good eats," will the fly extend its long sucking mouthtube, or *proboscis*. Extra taste hairs located at the tip of the fly's proboscis then become excited, causing the fly to suck up a tasty, nutritious meal of fresh animal dung or decaying plant or animal parts. Other favorite meals include leftover human foods such as blobs of maple syrup or chocolate cake.

Flies are not the only insects that taste their food with their feet. Bees and many butterflies share the ability and always put their feet first when it's time to eat.

HOW DOES A MOSQUITO FIND YOU IN THE DARK?

Darkness doesn't help us hide from hungry mosquitoes, because every time we breathe we give ourselves away! Female mosquitoes locate humans and other animal victims partly by sensing carbon dioxide, the waste gas we give off each time we let out a breath. Male mosquitoes, on the other hand, don't hunt for us. They don't need to because they eat only nectar and no blood.

If we could actually make ourselves stop breathing to get away from the predatory female mosquitoes, they would still be able to find us. This is because they also have special sensors on their antennae that detect body heat, sweat, and the odor of our skin. Researchers have demonstrated the remarkable sensing ability of these blood-thirsty creatures by pressing a hand against a clean glass plate, then inserting the plate into a cage full of female mosquitoes. Right away, many of them land on the spot that was touched and try to feed. In fact, their sensing power is so great, they will sometimes hang around the plate searching for the human for up to a half hour!

When they are out in the dark ready to feed, female mosquitoes first use their special sensing skills to see if there is a potential victim nearby. They do this by waving their antennae in all directions until they pick up a telltale odor or body heat. Once they detect the presence of a juicy dining opportunity, they turn their bodies until the signal being received by both antennae is equally strong. Then, they start flying toward the source of the warmth or smell. The hungry little insects keep adjusting the course as the signal gets stronger and stronger. Finally, they reach the target—a human or other creature containing blood. Of course, the next step is to zip in and grab a meal.

You may be wondering why female mosquitoes are so hungry for blood when the males aren't. The reason is that females must have a blood meal before they can produce eggs. Thus, they need it to contribute to the survival of their species.

HOW DO ANTS KNOW
WHEN YOU'RE HAVING A PICNIC?

You know what happens when you set out a picnic. First, there are one or two ants. Then, a few more appear. And soon ants are swarming everywhere carrying off your meal!

This happens because ants have a way of "telling" their nest mates that there's a new supply of food. These tiny insects also have the ability to direct their comrades right to site of it. Here's how they do it.

First, an ant that is out scouting for food happens to run across your picnic. Hurriedly, it picks up a tasty morsel and heads back to the nest. On the way, it marks its path by laying a special invisible "smell" trail. It does this by frequently pressing the back end of its body to the ground and releasing a scented chemical called a *pheromone*. Even though the trail is invisible, it points the way for other ants because they can follow the scent.

Once back home, the ant scurries about, tapping nest mates on the body or striking them with its antennae, front legs, or head. This makes the other ants excited and some of them run out of the nest. A number discover the scent trail and follow it right to your picnic. They collect morsels of food and head back home, leaving scent trails of their own.

Ants will keep coming and laying trails for other ants until the supply of food is gone. Then, they stop laying trails on their trip home. Since the trail is not renewed with more of the scented chemical, the odor begins to fade away. In just a few minutes, the trail—and the ants—are completely gone, too.

ARE ARMY ANTS REALLY KILLERS?

Army ants are like a huge, unstoppable killing machine. They sweep over the land in a great mass, grabbing up and killing any living thing that can't scramble or fly out of their path. Because they are meat-eaters with tremendous appetites, army ants hunt daily to feed the several hundred thousand or even twenty to thirty million members in their colony.

As their name suggests, these ferocious predators always work as a unit. When food is needed, thousands upon thousands of colony members go hunting together. Usually, they stream out in wide columns, with the ants in the back actually pushing the ones at the front forward. As the wall of ants advances it simply parts and encircles its prey. Any slow-moving, earth-bound creatures such as spiders, crickets, beetles, other ants, and small animals are trapped. The fearsome ants swarm in, grab the helpless victims in their jaws and then cover them with bites. Some species, called driver ants, use very strong hooklike jaw parts to rip their prey to pieces. These ants have even been known to devour large animals that were penned or hurt and unable to flee.

Within each army ant colony, there are actually several different forms, or castes, of ants. Most colonies have one very large queen whose main job is laying eggs. There are also a few large males to mate with the queen. All the other thousands or millions of colony members are workers. These range from very small ants that look after the queen and the young, medium-sized workers that go hunting, and large, ferocious soldiers that fight off enemies.

Unlike most kinds of ants, army ants don't build permanent nests and live in one place. Instead, they make a temporary home in a hollow log or crevice and stay for only a few weeks. This gives the queen time to lay eggs and the young ants, or larvae, time to become adults. To supply the colony with food, raiding parties go out hunting in the surrounding area each day.

Once the nesting period is over, the hungry horde goes on the march for a while. Each day is spent busily hunting, feeding, and then moving on. Late each night, the colony sets up a temporary camp and rests till morning. After several weeks of marching, the colony settles in one place again so the queen can lay another batch of eggs.

Because army ants mean death and destruction in the animal world, there are tales of them tracking down and killing humans. However, most scientists who have studied these insects in the wild feel the stories are exaggerated. They say that although the army ant's bite is extremely painful, it won't paralyze or kill people. Moreover, any person who can walk away briskly can escape an advancing column of ants. For one thing, the ants cannot "run" after their prey. For another, they lose track quickly if the victim swerves out of their way. This is because most army ants are blind! These predators hunt mainly by swarming over creatures that happen to be in their path or by following the scuffling sounds of victims trying to crawl away.

HOW DO GRASSHOPPERS HOP?

A grasshopper as big as a human could leap the length of a football field! The amazing jumping power of grasshoppers enables some of them to leap distances that are over ten times their own body lengths. These "supermen" of the insect world get their special jumping abilities from a pair of extra long and strong hind legs.

Like all insects, grasshoppers have six legs. The first four are short and ordinary. The back two legs, on the other hand, are so long that when they are fully stretched out they may be longer than the creature's entire body! These leaping legs are also equipped with thick, powerful muscles.

When a grasshopper wants to take off, it begins by bending its hind legs and pressing its *tarsi*, or footlike parts, against the ground. Then the insect uses a powerful contraction of its leg muscles to extend its long limbs, pushing itself up into the air.

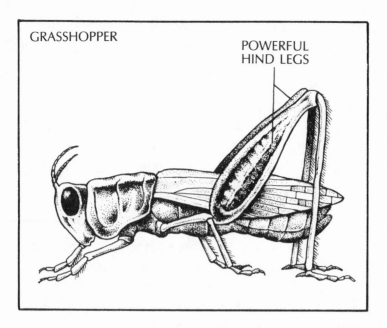

GRASSHOPPER

POWERFUL HIND LEGS

While a grasshopper can make real progress by leaping, covering several inches with each hop, a leap takes a lot of energy. Thus, grasshoppers don't jump unless they need to. The leggy insects generally make use of their high jump powers to get away from enemies, hurry toward a mate, or to prepare to take off in flight.

HOW DO CRICKETS CHIRP?

When a male cricket makes music, the sweet sounds don't come out of his mouth, they come from his wings! Each of the cricket's amazing wings carries a very special musical instrument. The instrument has two parts: a file, which consists of a row of tiny peglike bumps, and a hardened bar of skin called the scraper. When the scraper on one wing is rubbed against the file on the other, out comes a sharp, sweet chirp.

While a cricket's chirps may all sound the same to our ears, other crickets can pick out approximately four separate kinds of songs. Each song has its own unique pattern of chirps. In most cricket species these songs are sung solely by males.

Three of the six-legged musician's songs are sung during mating. They include a loud "calling song" which is used to attract females, a "courtship song" which encourages an interested female to mate, and an "after-mating song." A fourth "aggressive song" is produced by two male crickets when they are fighting.

Crickets cannot only vary the type of song that they produce, they can also change the speed at which they chirp it. Most crickets, however, only alter their chirping speed in response to changes in air temperature. One particular species, the snowy tree cricket, is so sensitive to temperature change that it has been called the "living thermometer." To find out the Fahrenheit temperature, a listener need only count the number of chirps produced by this cricket in fifteen seconds and add forty to it.

WHY DO FIREFLIES FLICKER?

Flickering on and off is the firefly's own special Morse code. Those beautiful lights you see twinkling in the air on a summer evening are really coded signals of fireflies advertising for a mate. A lightning bug's flickering pattern not only announces, "I'm available," but also tells what kind of firefly it is. Here's how the signaling works.

Each of the more than 130 kinds of fireflies in the world has its own special flashing code. The males of a particular species all send out a certain unique signal pattern—such as one long pulse every few seconds, or several quick flashes in a row. All females of the same species also have a unique answering pattern. For example, they may wait a certain number of seconds and send one quick flash, or they may pulse repeatedly.

This special set of signals, which scientists call a *species–specific code*, helps males and females of the same kind find one another in the night. A male firefly cruises about in the air, flashing his particular code in an effort to attract a female on the ground below. Instinctively, a female of his own species can pick out his advertisement from those of other males and then signal back that she is ready to mate.

While the species–specific flashing code is mainly a courtship aid, it also helps some predatory fireflies obtain their dinner! As remarkable as it sounds, the females in certain species "break the code" of the smaller varieties of lightning bugs they prey on and use it to lure unsuspecting males. First, the crafty predatory females look for the special flash code of potential male victims. Then they answer the male, imitating the signal of a female of his species. When the eager male zooms in close for mating, the large, hungry predator female is waiting to catch and eat him.

The trick doesn't always work, however. In regions where there are many predatory fireflies, the species they prey on learn to be careful. The potential male victims almost always approach answering females cautiously, to make sure they are interested in romance and not a meal. In this way, vulnerable males usually avoid getting caught.

Now that you know *why* fireflies flicker, you might also wonder *how* they manage to light up. The beautiful luminescent flashing is the result of a chemical reaction occurring in a part of the firefly's abdomen known as its lantern. Here, under the control of the insect's nervous system, a special substance called *luciferin* combines with oxygen and produces a glow. When this happens, the lantern gives off the bright flashes of light that we see in the night.

DO PRAYING MANTISES REALLY EAT THEIR MATES?

As awful as it seems to us, praying mantises will eat not only their mates, but their children if they get hungry enough! However, females don't normally devour their suitors and are not really any more bloodthirsty than the males.

Actually, the female mantis is usually friendly and non-threatening to her mate during courtship. The male begins to woo her by doing a little dance. Then, the female responds with a flirtatious mating dance of her own. In most cases, she doesn't attack her suitor and both parties come out of the romance very much alive.

Up until recently, scientists thought female mantises did usually eat their mates. They probably had this impression because mantises had only been studied in laboratories, not in the wild. In captivity, these insects have been known to chomp off the male's head during mating and then devour him. Some researchers think that this occurred because having an audience disturbed the females. Another possibility is that the captive insects were simply underfed and desperate for a meal. Mantises are such big eaters that they can put away up to fifteen full-grown crickets a day. After missing a few meals, a female is more interested in lunch than love!

WHY DOES THE PRAYING MANTIS LOOK LIKE IT'S PRAYING?

When a mantis lifts its front legs up, it isn't praying, it's "preying!" The large-eyed praying mantis uses its raised front legs as a special weapon for capturing insects and other tasty prey.

In order to catch a juicy insect, the mantis depends on ambushing techniques. This means that the large predator lies in wait and quickly lunges out to grab an unsuspecting victim passing by. To keep itself hidden, the mantis holds its body motionless. Its green or brown colors enable it to blend into the grass, bushes, or trees. Many man-

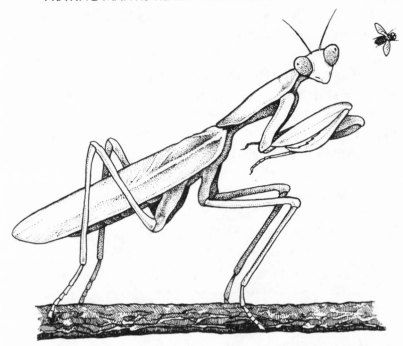

tids also have specially shaped, sticklike bodies, making them look very much like the leaves, twigs, or blades of grass on which they rest.

As it waits, the statuelike mantis rests on its four rear legs, holding its front legs folded up just under its head, in the distinctive "praying" position. When a small insect flits by, the mantis swiftly aims its mobile head at its target. Then, with lightning speed, the predator shoots its killing front legs toward the tiny insect. The capture takes the praying mantis less than half a second, and the skillful hunter rarely misses its mark.

Holding onto its squirming prize is no problem for the mantis. The large predator's front legs carry a row of sharp, piercing spines that grasp its meal tightly. The mantis also uses its super strong limbs to pull its prey to its mouth for chewing and swallowing.

HOW DO TERMITES EAT WOOD?

Even if our teeth were tough enough to chew wood, we humans couldn't make a meal of it. This is because humans and most other animals can't digest wood. The hungry little termite, however, finds wood, paper, linen, straw, and even leather very good food.

Wood and other termite foods all contain a tough, dry, substance called cellulose. Unlike most living things, the termite is able to break down woody cellulose and use it to provide energy. To perform this remarkable feat, the insignificant looking insect relies on help from some even smaller creatures called *protozoa*. These microscopic organisms live in the termite's gut and work along with their host to digest the woody food. Here's how the process works.

First, the termite chomps off a bite of its food using super-strong jaws with sharp sawing ridges. These chewing tools work so well that they can easily cut through hard wood, or even through lead pipe, if necessary.

Next, the food moves from the termite's mouthparts to a muscular section of its stomach called the gizzard. Here, it is ground into small particles. Finally, the particles go to the termite's gut, where they are acted upon by its digestive juices. At the same time, thousands and thousands of the protozoa swarm over the particles and release a chemical. This special chemical changes the cellulose into simple sugars and starches. These provide nourishment for both the termite and the protozoa.

You can probably see that the termite and the protozoa both benefit from their unusual relationship. The termite provides a steady supply of ground-up cellulose and a protected home for the protozoa. And the protozoa help turn cellulose particles into sugars and starches, which both they

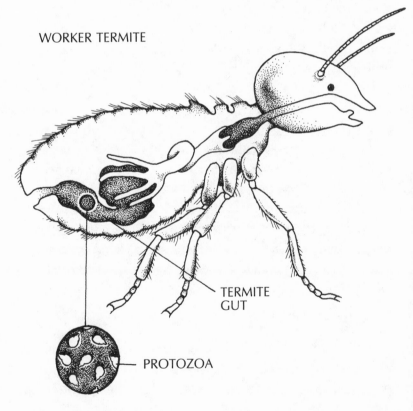

WORKER TERMITE

TERMITE GUT

PROTOZOA

and the termite can use for food energy. Scientists call such a mutually beneficial living arrangement between different kinds of organisms *symbiosis*.

WHY DO DRAGONFLIES HAVE BIG EYES?

A dragonfly uses over 56,000 tiny eyes to get a sharp view of its fast-moving insect prey. The tiny eyes, called facets, are actually bound together, in bundles of 28,000 to form the two giant compound eyes we notice.

Compound eyes, which resemble honeycombs, are found in many insects, but most are far smaller than the dragonfly's. A housefly for example has only five thousand facets per eye while an ant has around fifty. Neither of these insects seems to have the ability to see objects as clearly as the dragonfly. Instead, they depend upon their other senses, such as touch, taste, and smell, to locate food sources.

While the functioning of compound eyes is not completely understood, it is known that these specially designed light detectors are exceptionally good at seeing moving objects. For the dragonfly, which captures other insects in midair, the ability to notice movement is especially important.

Once a hungry dragonfly has used its good vision to spot its winged prey, the needle-shaped predator will then make use of its superior flying abilities to complete the capture. Moving at speeds of up to twenty-five miles per hour, the dragonfly

DRAGONFLY AND WATER STRIDERS

can swoop down on another insect and sweep the struggling animal up with its six, spike-studded legs. If the prey is a small insect, like a mosquito, the dragonfly will simply munch on its prize as it continues to fly along in search of the next victim. With a large catch, however, such as a bumblebee, the weighted-down hunter will be forced to land on the ground in order to savor its meal.

HOW CAN WATER STRIDERS WALK ON WATER?

If you could step off a stream bank and skate on the water's surface, you'd be a candidate for *The*

Guinness Book of World Records! Amazingly, however, this feat is so easy for the insects known as water striders that they spend most of their lives gliding around on ponds and streams.

Water striders, which look sort of like floating daddy longlegs (see page 40), not only catch their insect prey and eat it on the water, they also meet mates and carry out their courtship there as well. In addition, once a pair of striders has mated, the female even deposits her eggs on a floating leaf, piece of bark, feather, or other object. Clearly, water striders haven't much need to go on land. As a matter of fact, they don't go unless rain or strong wind stirs up the water surface or the water drops below 32 degrees Fahrenheit.

One reason water striders can so easily "walk" on their liquid environment is that they have specially designed bodies and legs. Their bodies are covered with water-repellent scales so they won't get heavy with water and sink. Also, their middle and back legs, which are the ones striders use for rowing and steering, are long and widely spaced. This arrangement spreads their weight over a larger area, so they don't push down hard enough in one spot to break through the water surface. In addition, the parts that actually touch the water, the feet and lower legs, are covered with unwettable hairs. These tiny hairs trap bubbles of air and work like mini-life preservers to buoy the striders up.

Another important reason striders can walk on water is that the water surface has a thin, strong, elastic film. Normally you don't see this film, but it's still there, helping to keep the striders afloat. The film forms because the very tiny parts, or molecules, that make up water tend to stick together when they contact the air.

If you want to prove the film exists, try this simple experiment. Set a glass on a flat surface and slowly pour water into the center of it. Being careful not to dribble down the side, continue adding water until the glass won't hold another drop. Next, look carefully at the glass from the side. You can see that the water actually rises above the rim. The water doesn't run out because the surface film is holding it in place.

WHY DO LOCUSTS ONLY COME OUT EVERY SEVENTEEN YEARS?

A hungry bird cannot depend upon a dinner that crawls out of the ground every seventeen years. Thus, the seventeen-year cicada (which was misnamed locust by early American pilgrims) avoids getting eaten by keeping its unprotected body hidden for long periods of time. In fact, this unusual insect spends almost its entire life as a youngster, or *nymph*, living underground where predators cannot get to it. Here, the young cicada feeds on the nutritious juices that it sucks from tree roots.

After seventeen years in its dark home the cicada crawls out into the air. Amazingly, along with it come thousands of other cicadas, all of whom are programmed in their genes to come out of the ground at almost the exact same time! The seemingly endless army of cicadas carpet the ground, bushes, and trees.

Once cicadas reach the surface of the ground, they squeeze out of their dry nymphal skins. Suddenly, they become winged, red-eyed adults, with the soft, juicy bodies birds love to eat. Now the fully mature insects perch on trees or take to the air to find mates. With only about three weeks left to live, the adult cicadas make short work of mating and egg laying. After this process is completed the insects finally die.

During the three short weeks of their adult lives, the cicadas provide a sudden wealth of food for birds and other predators. But even though the birds stuff themselves, they hardly make a dent in the huge population of the insects. There are just so many cicadas that large numbers manage to survive their predators. If the cicadas came out a few at a time, instead of all at once, then the birds could munch on a few insects every day and eventually eat most of them. But when they all appear at once, the birds can feed and feed, and a lot of the cicadas can still manage to remain uneaten.

DO JAPANESE BEETLES REALLY COME FROM JAPAN?

The Japanese beetles you see chomping away on plants in summer didn't just fly in from Japan, it was actually their ancestors who came purely by accident from the Orient to America. Before the twentieth century, there weren't any of these bronze- and green-colored insects in America. Then, in 1917, a few Japanese beetles were found in a nursery in Pennsylvania, apparently sent to the United States along with a shipment of plants from Japan.

Nobody realized that these uninvited guests would spread rapidly and do so much damage to our crops and gardens. In Japan and China, where the beetles were native, they were not abundant or troublesome at all. So no one in this country took steps to get rid of them early on.

Just three years after they arrived, however, the beetles had dramatically increased in numbers and had already spread almost fifty miles from the nursery site. Entomologists now knew they had a problem, but there were simply too many of the little pests to get rid of by using insecticide or catching them in traps.

The entomologists eventually realized that the overpopulation by the beetles had occurred because they didn't have many natural enemies in the United States. In Japan, there were certain wasps, flies, and worms that preyed on the beetles and kept them from becoming too numerous. Here, however, there weren't enough predators to keep them in check. Bringing the Japanese beetle into our country had upset what scientists call the " *ecological balance*," the delicate set of relationships that exists among all the plants and animals and their surroundings.

Restoring the balance so Japanese beetles don't "take over" is a process that is still going on today. American scientists have imported some of the enemies that prey on the beetles in Asia. They have also studied the idea of introducing diseases that might infect the plant-eating pests. Unfortunately, however, these natural enemies don't seem to do as well in the United States as the beetles. Thus, Japanese beetles continue to multiply and spread. In some years and locations, there are so many that they swarm in and strip all the leaves from trees or crops in just a few minutes.

American experts learned a hard lesson from our problem with the Japanese beetle. Nowadays, great care is taken not to let any foreign insects—even ones that seem harmless—into our country. And those that do slip in are quickly stamped out *before* harm is done.

WHY IS IT SO HARD TO GET RID OF ROACHES?

A very hungry cockroach will dine on glue! It may also make a meal of soap, wallpaper, television cords, and other seemingly indigestible objects. If things get really bad, this almost indestructible insect can even live without any food at all for as long as three months!

The roach's unusual feeding habits are just one of the things that enable this quick-moving creature to survive, and survive, and survive. The

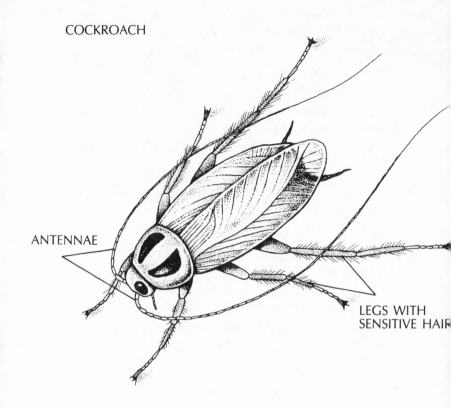

COCKROACH

ANTENNAE

LEGS WITH
SENSITIVE HAIR

pesky insect has a very sensitive body that's designed to make it almost unkillable. One special feature is the four fat feelers, called palpi, which dangle below the cockroach's mouth. Tiny hairs that cover the feelers are sensitive to taste, odor, and touch. These hairs enable the roach to pretaste food, before eating it. Thus, anything that tastes like it might be poisonous can be avoided.

Cockroaches also possess knowledgeable knees! Special movement detectors in the insect's knee joints allow it to not only pick up the strong vibrations of a human's foot steps, but also the delicate vibrations produced by another skittering cockroach out searching for a mate.

The roach's ability to avoid predators is further increased by the insect's special breeze detector. Pointy feelers called cerci, which stick out of the animal's back end, can sense even the slight draft of air a human might create while attempting to sneak up on the roach. The roach is so alert that, when its cerci detect movements, the speedy insect can take off in fifty-four thousandths of a second. That's less time than it would take you to blink your eye! No wonder it's so hard to squash a roach.

As a final insurance against humans and other predators, roaches can produce young in incredibly large numbers. A single pair of German roaches (which are the common U.S. roach) can, for example, produce over 400,000 children, grandchildren, great-grandchildren, etc., in just one year!

Now, all this doesn't mean that humans have no weapons to use against the roach. The insects can be tricked into eating certain poisons. Also, some substances like boric acid (used by humans as an eyewash), can destroy the waterproof wax that coats the cockroach's body, causing the insect to shrivel up and die.

No matter what we do, though, we're not likely to ever be totally free from the presence of the roach. The best evidence of the insect's ability to survive can be found by looking at the past. It seems that roaches have been around for over 300 million years. That makes this group of animals at least 298 million years older than man.

ARE ALL LADYBUGS FEMALE?

Despite their name, some ladybugs are actually "men bugs" and not ladies! Ladybugs come in two sexes just like other kinds of insects, because both males and females are needed to produce offspring.

Not only aren't all ladybugs "ladies," but these black-spotted red beetles don't act at all cute or "ladylike" either. In fact, these colorful creatures are fierce, hungry predators of other insects. They will dine on just about any insect that they are big enough to kill. Their favorite foods are mealybugs and tiny plant-eating insects called aphids. The ever-hungry ladybugs have been known to gobble up one hundred aphids a day!

Though they may not look it, ladybugs are quite well-designed for hunting and feeding. Their jaws are strong and fitted with claw-like parts called pincers. These are used to grab and hold onto aphids and other victims. The hungry little beetles also have a very efficient way of devouring their prey. First, they bore a hole in the victim's body. Next, they squirt a special liquid into the hole. This fluid dissolves and digests the victim's insides, which the ladybugs can simply suck up into their own bodies. They don't even have to bother chewing their food!

In case you're still wondering why these predatory beetles got the name ladybug, there *is* a good reason. During earlier times in Europe, these insects were dedicated to the Virgin Mary and called

"Beetles of Our Lady" because they helped protect vineyards from attacks from aphids.

WHY DO LICE LIVE IN PEOPLE'S HAIR?

If you're going to suck someone's blood, it's a good idea to keep yourself hidden from them. Blood sucking human lice thus make their homes on places where they aren't likely to be found. These irritating insects hide themselves on heads, in armpits, and in creases of clothing. In fact, they will lodge their tiny bodies anywhere that nice thick growths of hair, or layers of clothing, hide and protect them from being picked off by human fingers.

There are actually several different kinds of lice that feed on human blood. The lice that live on people's heads are different from cooties, which are lice that prefer to crawl around people's bodies. Although these two kinds make their homes on different parts of the body, they still have a lot in common.

To keep themselves from falling off their human hosts, for example, both kinds have specially designed grasping legs. At the tip of each leg is a long claw and a thumblike knob. The claw and the knob can be closed against each other in order to lock onto a slippery strand of hair or a piece of cloth.

Once it has found itself a human host, a louse will move toward the person's skin in order to obtain a meal. The well-equipped insect carries a pair of sharp-tipped rods or stylets, which it uses to pierce the human's skin. Then, the louse holds its stylets together to form a sucking tube. It is through this tiny straw that the hungry animal sucks up its blood dinner.

Not only do head lice live in human hair, they also lay their eggs there. Each egg or nit is covered with a special glue that sticks it to a strand of hair. The glue holds the nits so tightly they won't come off even during shampooing.

Usually, lice get passed from one human to another only when the two individuals touch. One reason for this is that lice cannot live without blood for more than three days. Thus they won't risk leaving one juicy human host unless another is right near by. Furthermore, lice cannot fly to a new host, because like fleas and many other blood suckers, they lack wings. The slow-moving lice must instead use their claw-footed legs to crawl from host to host.

Because it is less than one quarter of an inch long, a single louse doesn't do much damage when it sucks blood from a human. Large numbers of these tiny creatures, however, can cause weakness and intense itching in their human victim. The real danger of lice, though, arises from the fact that they occasionally carry diseases such as typhus from human to human. In some instances, thousands of humans have died due to illnesses spread by lice.

Good hygiene is the best way to keep from getting lice. Unfortunately however, even someone who is very clean can pick up a bunch of these nasty little insects from someone else who has them. Luckily, there are special steps available to help get rid of any lice that find their way onto a human's body.

WHY DO BEDBUGS LIVE IN BEDS?

If you thought human blood was really delicious and especially liked sneaking your meals in the dark, it would make sense to hang around a bed. Well, that's exactly what bedbugs do. They stick around waiting for the bed's occupant to tuck in so they can grab a bite!

Actually, though, bedbugs don't spend most of their time in beds. After biting a sleeping victim and slurping up as much blood as they can hold, the stuffed little insects usually spend the next week or so in cracks or other dark places digesting their meal. Then, they return to the place where they're likely to find more food—the bed.

Bedbugs can be very patient about waiting, too. If the person they dine on happens to go away, they can survive for several months without eating. They have also been known to live on mice when no human beings were available.

Most people know about bedbugs from the old rhyme, "Good night, sleep tight. Don't let the bedbugs bite!" However, due to modern insecticides and better sanitation today, the pesky little creatures aren't too common in the United States any more. If you ever *do* happen to see some of these small, flat, reddish-brown bugs scurrying around

BED BUG

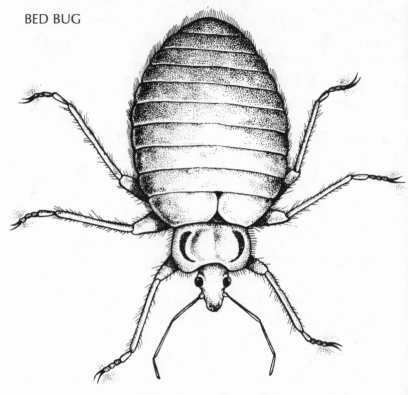

ABOUT 10X ACTUAL SIZE

your sheets or mattress, though, try not to get upset. They aren't dangerous and don't cause disease. Also the bites don't hurt, although they may leave a red, itchy bump on the skin.

CAN PEOPLE GET FLEAS?

They certainly can. In fact, if you discover a bunch of small, itchy red bumps on your skin, and you have a pet dog or cat, there's a good chance that you have flea bites. Furthermore, the flea that bit you is probably the common cat flea.

Like all of the 1,500 different species of fleas in the world, cat fleas feed on blood. Despite their name, cat fleas seem to be equally fond of cats and dogs. A hungry cat flea will also take its meal from a nice, juicy human.

If your house has fleas, you'll have a hard time keeping them from finding you. Fleas have a number of remarkable ways of tracking down humans and other mammals. These amazing little insects can sense the waste gas, carbon dioxide, that comes from your nose each time you breathe out. They are also sensitive to the movements of air that are caused by your moving body. Once the flea discovers that you are a tasty host animal, it hops onto you to get its meal.

ADULT FLEA

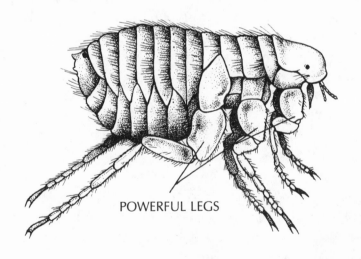

POWERFUL LEGS

ABOUT 20X ACTUAL SIZE

If you've ever seen fleas, you've probably noticed that you never actually see the little pests flitting around in the air. The reason for this is that fleas don't fly. They can't fly, because their bodies are flat and wingless. This enables them to slip readily through the thick fur of a mammal or the dense feathers of a bird, without having bothersome wings to get in the way.

To get onto their hosts, fleas use six long powerful legs. Thick leg muscles enable these mighty jumpers to leap as high as twelve inches into the air. That's quite a feat for an insect that's less than one-eighth of an inch in length. If we humans could jump as well for our size, a six-foot man could leap 576 feet!

If you've got fleas in your house you won't get rid of them by going away on vacation. These blood suckers are very patient when it comes to waiting for a meal. Some fleas can live for over a year without feeding! Getting rid of fleas may require using insecticides and thoroughly cleaning your house and pets.

WHY ARE BUTTERFLIES' WINGS SO COLORFUL?

The beautiful, eye-catching orange and black coloring of a monarch butterfly is really a warning of danger! Like a red flag, it tells birds: *Poisonous—do not take a bite!*

Because monarchs are poisonous, a bird that makes the mistake of eating one may vomit and become ill. After this awful experience the bird usually decides to avoid those nasty-tasting orange and black butterflies in the future.

The monarch's warning colors not only help it, but they also aid another orange and black butterfly called the viceroy. The viceroy isn't poisonous and it isn't related to a monarch. However, it mimics, or looks almost like, one. As a result, birds and other predators think the viceroy *is* a monarch and leave it alone, too.

There are other beautiful butterflies, and in each case their particular appearance helps them to survive as well. Sometimes, the bright colors or markings simply help a butterfly attract a mate. More often, though, they provide protection against enemies. For example, the adonis butterfly and many other members of a family called blues are a lovely, silvery shade of blue. This color catches *our* attention, but scientists have discovered that *birds* don't see blue very well. Thus, their color enables blues to blend into the sky and surroundings and to avoid birds.

The vivid tiger- or zebra-striped markings of swallowtail butterflies protect them in a similar way. Researchers have found that such stripes and lines tend to trick the eye and make the whole body appear as separate parts. Scientists call this strange effect *disruptive coloration*. Because of it, predators tend to see a jumble of confusing pieces, rather than a juicy swallowtail flitting by.

Brightly colored wings spots like those on the buckeye, painted lady, and a number of other butterflies also help trick predators. In some cases,

MONARCH

THICK BAND

2 ROWS OF SPOTS

CAN YOU FIND THE
DIFFERENCES BETWEEN THE BUTTERFLIES?

VICEROY

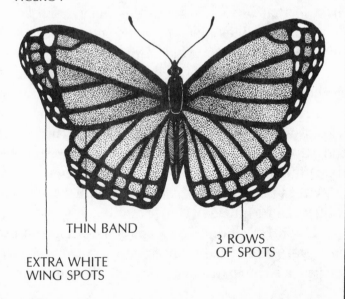

THIN BAND

3 ROWS OF SPOTS

EXTRA WHITE WING SPOTS

when the spots are large and look like owl eyes, they tend to startle and frighten birds. When the spots are small and look like insect eyes, birds have trouble finding a butterfly's real eyes. This creates problems because birds normally strike at the victim's head in order to kill it instantly. If a bird is tricked and pecks at an eye spot instead, the victim has a chance to escape with just a chunk out of its wing!

Of course, not all butterflies have flashy colors or beautiful markings. In fact, most of the 24,000 different kinds are fairly plain. Many are designed to blend into their environment and look like tree bark, brown leaves, faded flowers or other parts of the background. Predators have a hard time seeing butterflies that look so much like the scenery around them. We have trouble seeing them too. That's why we only tend to notice the beautiful, brightly-colored butterflies in the world.

WHY DO BUTTERFLIES BEGIN LIFE AS CATERPILLARS?

The butterfly is like two insects in one. It begins life as a wiggly caterpillar, perfectly designed for eating, and ends life as colorful adult, built for flying and finding a mate. The young, larval butterfly can devote all its energy to its main task, feeding and growing. The adult butterfly, on the other hand, can rid itself of all those now unnecessary feeding parts, develop wings, and put its energy into its main job, mating and reproducing.

When the butterfly first hatches out of its egg as a caterpillar, it is little more than a multilegged feeding machine. The tiny creature lacks wings and it doesn't move about very much. Its main purpose in life is to eat and grow. This task is made easy by the fact that a female butterfly lays her eggs on a type of plant that her young like to eat. Thus, when the caterpillar emerges from its egg it is surrounded by an abundant supply of good food. Using strong chewing mouthparts, the ever-hungry insect can gnaw away at any nearby leaves or stems. By stuffing itself with nutrients, the caterpillar gets ready to become an adult.

In order to turn into a butterfly, the caterpillar must redesign its body. It must reform its mouth and legs, and grow wings. To make these changes, the caterpillar stops eating and enters a new stage in its life. It becomes a hard, motionless pupa. The pupa is created when the caterpillar wraps itself in a tight cocoon spun from its own silk glands. Gradually, over a period of several days, the seemingly motionless pupa or chrysalis magically changes into a colorful winged adult, or butterfly.

Beautifully transformed, the delicate butterfly breaks out of its cocoon and enters a new part of its life. The freshly formed adult has lost its ability to chew and has replaced its old larval mouth parts with a long, coiled tube. Called the proboscis, this strawlike tube is used by the delicate insect to suck up its new food source, the nectar of flowers. Feeding, however, is so unimportant to these adult butterflies that some species lack any mouthparts and

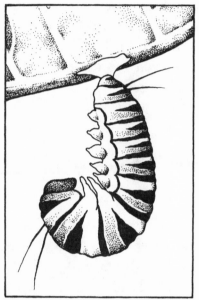

1

CATERPILLAR
ABOUT TO
SPIN CHRYSALIS

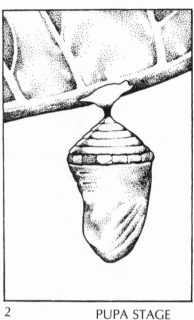

2   PUPA STAGE

3

NEWLY EMERGED
MONARCH BUTTERFLY

Why Do Butterflies Begin Life as Caterpillars? . . . **59**

are not able to feed at all! Whether or not they can feed, all butterflies have the same main goal, to fly off in search of a mate. In addition, females must locate exactly the right place for laying their eggs. They search for a special type of plant that will provide the right kind of food for their offspring and deposit their eggs on it. Their life's work done, many butterflies then simply die.

WHY DO TENT CATERPILLARS MAKE TENTS?

Tent caterpillars build tents for the same reason that human campers pitch them. They want protection from rain, cold, wind, and hot sun. The little moth larvae also use their sticky, weblike tent to hide from enemies such as birds.

Tent building is a family affair. All the brothers and sisters that come from one batch of tent caterpillar moth eggs work together to construct their shelter. Immediately after hatching in the spring, the fifty to one hundred fifty or so larvae begin to build. The little caterpillars construct their tent with silk released from special mouthparts. Usually the tent is placed on the same fork of the fruit tree where their mother deposited her eggs the preceding fall.

Once the handy structure is completed, the caterpillars divide their time between resting together in their community home and munching on leaves in nearby branches. At the start of a feeding period all the larvae crawl out to eat at once. The

TENT CATERPILLARS

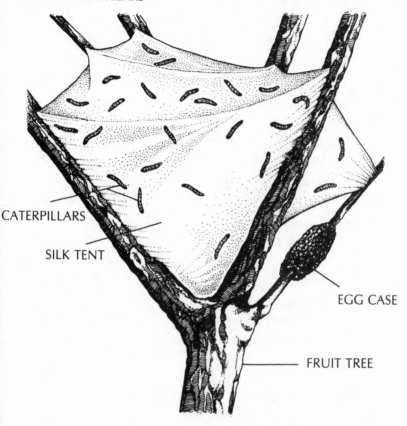

CATERPILLARS

SILK TENT

EGG CASE

FRUIT TREE

hungry creatures don't waste time searching for food on branches they have already stripped of leaves. Instead, they go right to ones with lots of foliage.

Scientists say the caterpillars can do this because they leave thin silken trails wherever they go. When a larva returns home from a branch that still has plenty of leaves, it adds a special chemical, or pheromone, to its silk thread. This tells its tent mates, "Good food this way!" However, when the creature returns from an area that has been stripped bare, it doesn't add this chemical message. Its brothers and sisters can tell by the unmarked trail that the spot has already been visited and that the food is probably gone.

For about a month or more, the tent caterpillars march out to eat several times a day. After each feeding they return to the shelter of the tent to rest and digest their leafy dinner. Eventually, when they are about two inches long, they leave their comfortable home for good. Each one goes off alone to seek a crevice or other private spot. There it wraps itself in a silken case, or cocoon. The insects spend the summer lying inside their cocoons, quietly changing from larvae into moths. In fall, they emerge as adult moths and fly out to find mates. Finally, the females lay their eggs in the forks or branches of fruit trees, thus insuring that a new batch of tent makers can appear in spring.

WHY DO INCHWORMS INCH?

The inchworm would be the hands-down winner of the caterpillar derby! Though these insects, which are actually moth larvae, appear slow moving to us, their looping style of walking makes them far faster than other caterpillars.

The inchworm's strange inching crawl results from the fact that these unusual moth larvae have legs at each end, but none in the middle. While most caterpillars have eight pairs of legs, spaced along the length of their bodies, inchworms have only five.

For the inchworm, moving forward involves two basic steps. First, it pulls its rear end forward toward its head, making its middle into a loop. Next it raises its front end, stretching ahead toward its goal. In contrast, other caterpillars plod along lifting one pair of legs after another all the way down their length.

Naturally, inchworms and other caterpillars do not keep all those extra legs when they turn into moths and butterflies. Like other insects, inchworms have only three pairs of legs in their adult form.

ARE THERE REALLY WORMS THAT MAKE SILK?

Yes *and* no! There are insects called silkworms and they do make silk. However, they are

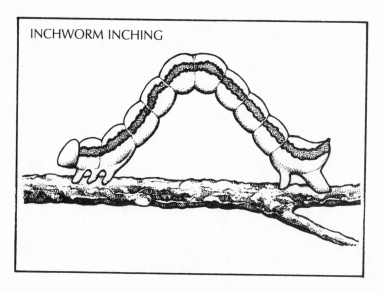

INCHWORM INCHING

not really worms, but caterpillars, or larvae, of the silk moth. The silk moth caterpillars are so good at making silk that each one can spin a strand more than half a mile long!

The Chinese have been raising silk moths for their precious thread since about 1800 B.C. Silk farmers carefully guarded their techniques for hundreds of years. Then, in the sixth century A.D., several monks smuggled out some silkworms and a supply of their food to Europe. Soon the amazing secret of how to make silk was known everywhere. But today, the Chinese and Japanese are still the largest producers of silk.

Modern silk farming is a year-round operation that takes place indoors. Here's how it's done.

Silk farming begins with special moths that are raised and kept in cages. Most silk farmers choose a cream-colored species called the cultivated silk moth. This particular weaver produces long strands and a very high-quality fabric.

Every autumn, the farmers start getting ready for the next year's silkworm crop by allowing some of the adult moths to mate and the females to lay their eggs. The farmers then place these eggs in refrigerators to prevent them from hatching out during the winter. This step is important because cultivated silk moth caterpillars eat only fresh mulberry leaves and these aren't available in winter.

In spring, when the mulberry trees begin to grow new leaves, the farmers warm up the eggs and let them hatch. The tiny caterpillars that emerge are pale whitish-green and wormlike in appearance. They are placed in huge trays and given all the fresh mulberry leaves they can eat. The hungry little weavers spend the next month munching away and getting larger.

When the silkworms are about three inches long, they are ready to wrap themselves in cocoons, or to *pupate*. In nature, the pupal stage is important because it gives the caterpillars time to reshape their bodies and develop into adult moths. To silk farmers, it's important because this is when the caterpillars actually spin their silk. They do this by releasing a continuous strand through parts on their lower jaws called spinnerets and weaving the strand around themselves to form a cocoon.

If left to themselves, the pupae would eventually develop into moths. However, before this can happen, the farmers "harvest" their silk crop by killing most of the pupae. This prevents the moths inside from breaking out of their cocoons and cutting the strand. The farmers collect the silk by unwinding the long strand of each cocoon. These are washed and four or five of the thin strands are caught up together and twisted into thread. A few pupae are saved and allowed to become moths so there will be eggs for the next crop of silkworms. The farmers raise about four crops every spring and summer.

Cultivated silk moths have been bred and raised by man for so many centuries that the species could no longer survive in the wild. The adult moths have lost their ability to fly and the caterpillars are not able to search out their own food. In fact, the insects are so completely dependent on humans that they would probably become extinct if we didn't need them to produce the beautiful fabric called silk.

WHY DO MOTHS FLY INTO THE LIGHT?

Surprising as it may sound, moths aren't really attracted to light. A moth flies into a light bulb or candle because it can't help it! Somehow, the brightness confuses the creature's sense of direction and it can't fly straight anymore.

Scientists still don't completely understand why a nearby light causes this reaction in the moth. They do know that, unlike human beings, the moth uses light rays from the moon or sun as a guide when it flies. The moth keeps itself moving in a straight line by constantly checking its position against the angle of the light rays striking its eyes.

Although this complicated guidance system works fine when the light source is far away, it obviously goes haywire when the light is close by. Stimulated by the nearby bulb or candle, the moth's nervous system directs its body to fly so that both eyes receive the same amount of light. This locks the helpless creature onto a course toward the light and eventually causes it to blunder right into the bulb or flame.

You may wonder why the moth doesn't save itself by closing its eyes and blocking out the light rays that are drawing it toward destruction. The fact is, it can't, because moths, like other insects, don't have eyelids!

WHY DO DADDY LONGLEGS HAVE SUCH LONG LEGS?

Scientists aren't really sure why the spiderlike daddy longlegs (also known as the harvestmen) walk on eight remarkably long limbs. Some experts think that stiltlike legs enable these unusual creatures to take long strides. This makes it easier for the fast-moving predators to cover a lot of ground in their search for insect prey. In contrast, there are a number of species of short-legged harvestmen. These forms tend to be slower and less active than their long-legged cousins.

Other scientists suggest that long legs enable harvestmen to sneak up on their tiny insect prey. The mites and other little insects that provide food for the daddy longlegs may only notice a single long leg approaching. One leg doesn't look like a dangerous enemy and wouldn't scare the insects away. The daddy longlegs can readily pounce on the unsuspecting prey below.

A third theory is that eight long legs make a wonderful fence that provides a special kind of protection for a daddy longlegs. Using legs that can be as much as thirty times longer than their bodies, daddy longlegs can often keep themselves well out of the reach of a hungry predator.

As handy as they are, a daddy longlegs' legs are sometimes more useful off the body than they are on it. Like its shorter-legged relatives, the spiders, the daddy longlegs has a habit of throwing off a leg in order to protect its body.

Leg throwing, a behavior which scientists call *autotomy*, occurs when a predator gets too close or grabs at a limb. The daddy longlegs can break off the trapped leg and run off to safety on the other seven. Meanwhile, the discarded leg has a life all its own. Even though it's no longer attached to its owner it continues to wiggle about on the ground! This moving leg confuses a predator and allows the daddy longlegs time to escape.

Although loss of a leg may seem horrible to us, it's not a big deal for the daddy longlegs. With so many legs to begin with, this speedy creature can spare one or two. The daddy longlegs can move very well using just six or seven of its skinny limbs. Furthermore, if the animal is still young, it can actually grow a new leg to replace the one it lost.

HOW CAN TICKS HANG ON SO TIGHT?

If you've ever tried to remove a tick from your dog, you probably noticed that these tiny eight-legged bloodeaters seem to stick like glue. In fact, although dog ticks are usually smaller than a baby's fingernail, they can be hard for even a full-grown human being to pull off! That's because these insignificant-looking creatures are uniquely designed to lock on to a host animal and stay there until they finish their meal.

One special design feature that helps ticks hold on tight is a protruding mouth part called a *hypostome*. This handy structure contains row after row of barblike teeth that the hungry parasite inserts through the victim's skin. The rows of teeth are angled so they slip in easily, but like fishhook barbs, they catch and hold in the flesh if pulled backwards.

As added insurance against being removed from its prey, the dog tick carries along a personal supply of cement! Once the bloodeater begins its meal, its mouthparts release this sticky substance into the wound and over the victim's skin. Very

TICK'S MOUTHPARTS

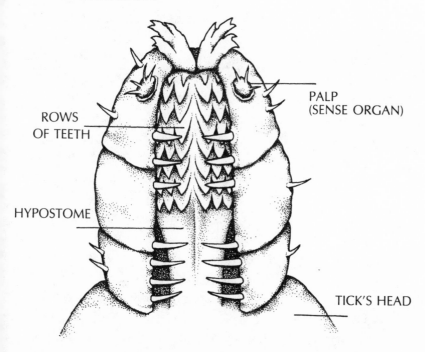

ROWS OF TEETH

PALP (SENSE ORGAN)

HYPOSTOME

TICK'S HEAD

How Can Ticks Hang on So Tight? . . . **69**

soon the cement hardens, fixing the diner tightly to its feeding place. Then, the hungry parasite eats and eats, often swelling up to ten times its original size!

Of course, nobody likes to have dinner interrupted, but the greedy little tick has a special reason for wanting to stick around until it's completely stuffed. A huge blood meal is needed before female ticks can develop eggs and produce more ticks. So, the ability to hang on tight during feeding is important in insuring the survival of the tick species.

HOW DO SPIDERS BUILD WEBS?

The beautiful spiral webs that catch our eye on a dewy morning are the work of a very special group of spiders. These master weavers are called orb web spiders. Orb web builders are unique because, while all spiders can produce silken threads, not all create webs. Even those species that do build webs often put together the rather sloppy tangles of threads that we notice in the corners of our homes. None can match the tidy, intricate patterns designed by the orb web spiders.

Like all spiders, the orb builder is a marvelous web-making machine. In fact, it has all the tools needed for web building packed neatly into its body. For example, the spider's back end houses a collection of silk glands that produce liquid silk. A spider squeezes or pulls the silk out of its body through tiny tubes called spinnerets. The pulling of the liquid silk transforms it into hard silken

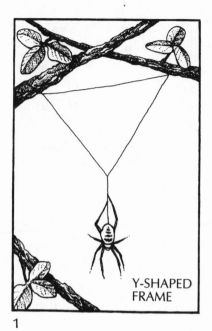

ORB WEB SPIDER
BUILDING WEB

RING OF SPOKES
MADE OF
NON-STICKING
THREADS

Y-SHAPED
FRAME

1

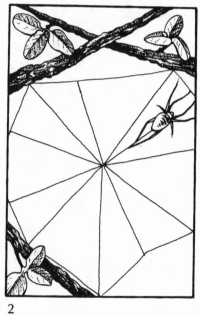

2

3

SPIRAL OF
STICKY THREADS

How Do Spiders Build Webs? . . . **71**

threads. Newly formed threads are both tough and elastic. They do a wonderful job of supporting the weight of the spider.

Eight long legs with claws are another part of the spider's web-making machine. These super-sensitive limbs enable the tiny weaver to feel its way along its web, measure the distances between threads, and draw out its long silk strands.

An orb web spider puts together its neatly patterned web in a series of steps. The eight-legged builder begins by putting down a support structure of nonsticky threads. It is on this support that the spider moves as it constructs the heart of the web, the sticky spiral. The neatly coiled loops of the sticky spiral form a trap to catch any insects that happen to fly into it.

The orb-spider starts its web by extending a Y-shaped frame of threads between tree twigs or branches. Then, the spider strengthens the delicate frame by surrounding it with a box of threads. Next, the tiny artist lays out a ring of spokes that spread from the center of the web like the rays of the sun. While the spider lays down the spokes, it also begins to build a temporary spiral. The temporary spiral is a continuous ring of threads that helps to hold the spokes in place. Finally, the spider completes the web by creating a spiral of sticky threads. As it does this, the little weaver removes the temporary spiral. Once the web is completed, the spider moves to the center of the silken trap or to a nearby hiding place to wait for a tasty insect.

Althought the orb web looks like a thoughtfully designed structure, the spider creates it by instinct. All the information that the careful builder needs to properly lay out its threads is already present in the spider's little brain. The orb weaver spiderling can build a perfect web on its first try and it never has to practice!

The entire process of building a web takes the spider less than one hour. It's a good thing too, because many orb weavers build a new web every day. Weaving so many webs requires a lot of silk and in order not to be wasteful, the thrifty orb web spider often eats its old web before it begins a new one.

WHY DOESN'T A SPIDER GET STUCK IN ITS WEB?

Slippery legs are the reason that a spider can stay unstuck! Using its eight oil-coated limbs, a spider can speed over the sticky threads that swirl in a spiral at the center of its web.

Although the spider doesn't get caught in the sticky spiral that it uses to trap insects, this particular predator still avoids crossing the gluey lines most of the time. Possibly, if the spider did step on the slippery threads with oily legs, it would make the lines lose some of their stickiness.

A spider can usually stay off the sticky areas because a web actually has two parts. It includes a framework of dry, slippery threads that spread out like spokes, and the central spiral of sticky threads. (See "How Do Spiders Build Webs?" for details.) When the spider walks, it moves mainly along the dry slippery threads. The tiny tightrope walker keeps from slipping by grasping the slick silk strands with the curved claws that extend from its legs. When at rest, the spider hangs in the center of the web, holding its body outward, away from the gluey spiral. In this way, the little predator is ready to pounce on a juicy insect that gets snagged in the web's sticky strands.

HOW DO SPIDERS CATCH INSECTS?

A spider's web is like the world's finest catcher's mitt. Not only does it catch insects on its sticky strands, but it holds onto them until the hungry spider can get to its wiggly meal.

While there are lots of different kinds of insect-trapping spider webs, the orb web is one of the most intricate. The special catching features of this web are best understood by looking at the way that an orb web spider captures its prey.

The hungry orb spider normally rests quietly at the center, or hub, of its web, awaiting the arrival of its next meal. When a fly or other insect gets snagged in the sticky strands, it struggles, causing the threads of the web to vibrate. Of course, the waiting predator can feel these vibrations immediately. Using its long legs, the spider then plucks the radiating strands of its web. This plucking is not meant for making music! It helps the spider to tell which threads are heavy with the weight of its prey.

You may wonder why the orb spider uses its super-sensitive legs to locate its prey rather than its eight eyes. One reason for this is that, despite all those eyes, these spiders tend to be near-sighted and are much better at detecting things by touch. (In contrast, hunting spiders, which catch their prey without webs, have very good vision and do all their hunting by sight.)

Once the orb spider has located its victim the speedy predator rushes along its web toward the catch. The spider must be fast, because within a few seconds a little fly could free itself from the sticky trap.

To secure its prey, the spider moves in and wraps some of its silk threads around the victim. Next, when the struggling prey is completely tied up, the leggy predator bites its prize. Poison from the bite paralyzes the victim and keeps it from wiggling free. Now, the spider has plenty of time to feed and can afford to be particular about where it eats. Orb spiders always move their silk wrapped package to the "dining room," or hub of the web. Here, a spider can readily detect the arrival of any other insects that might blunder into its web during mealtime.

The spider eats its meal in a rather incredible way. Instead of chewing up and then digesting food inside its body, like we do, the spider digests food outside its body! First the predator uses its strong jaws, or *chelicera*, to crush the body of its prey. Then it simply squirts digestive juices onto its mashed-up meal. Finally, it uses its mouth parts to suck up the dissolved insect!

CAN BLACK WIDOW SPIDERS REALLY KILL PEOPLE?

The black widow spider carries a powerful poison making it a very dangerous human pest. Because the tiny male black widows do not bite, it is only the larger black females that are a threat to humans.

The black widow spider can be identified by the bright red patch on its shiny black belly (naturally, however, you'd never want to turn one over to check!). This fearsome spider produces what is believed to be the most powerful poison in the animal world. Also, when it bites, the wound is extremely painful. Within a short period of time, the black spider's poison can cause nausea, vomiting, difficulty in breathing, and a variety of other very unpleasant symptoms. In a few rare cases, the black widow's venom has even caused death.

Despite its nasty bite, the black widow spider is a shy creature. It will sit quietly on the web that it constructs and await the arrival of a tasty insect. A native of the eastern United States, Canada, and Mexico, this spider often makes its home in people's garages, garbage dumps, and outhouses. Fortunately, this dangerous creature rarely bites and it doesn't go out of its way to attack humans. In fact, it is only when the half inch female gets squeezed accidentally against a human's body or is threatened that it will inject its horrible venom.

ARE TARANTULAS DANGEROUS?

The large, hairy creatures we call tarantulas look pretty scary, but they are not really dangerous to humans. Although these giants of the spider world can use their sharp-pointed mouth parts, or *chelicera*, to pierce a person's skin, the bite is not deadly. Though at first the bite is painful, like a wasp sting, the pain usually fades within an hour.

For some other members of the animal kingdom, though, a tarantula bite can be not only painful, but also quite deadly. The poison injected by the fierce-looking spider can kill an insect, a frog, a snake, or even a small bird. Most American tarantulas live on the ground and prey on insects. A few tropical South American forms live in trees and prefer to dine on the larger frogs and birds.

There are about thirty different species of tarantulas living in the dry regions of the Southwestern United States. Even if you live in tarantula country, however, there's little chance that one of the leggy creatures will attack you. These hairy spiders only bite humans if they are teased or feel threatened. In fact, tarantulas are easily tamed and some people consider them rather nice pets!

DOES A MILLIPEDE REALLY HAVE A MILLION LEGS?

It wouldn't take you all day to count a millipede's legs. It wouldn't even take you an hour!

Although the animal's name might suggest that it has a million legs, in fact the number of limbs on a millipede won't even total a thousand. Despite the fact that the word millipede means "thousand-legged," these many-limbed creatures actually have less than two hundred legs in all. Of course, two hundred is still a lot of legs!

It may surprise you to learn that all those legs don't help the millipede move very quickly. In fact, just the opposite is true. Millipedes are very slow, far slower than centipedes, which usually have around fifty legs.

So why have all those legs if they don't get your body going at top speeds? Lots of limbs are good for pushing. They enable the millipede to hold its body stiffly as it tunnels through piles of leaves and dirt in search of the decaying plants and animals on which it feeds. The leaves not only provide the millipede with food, they also create a good hiding place for the slow-moving creature.

Even a well-hidden millipede, however, may be dug out from its cover by a resourceful predator. Since its many legs won't help it scurry quickly away from the danger, the millipede has evolved several methods to avoid getting eaten. When disturbed, the creature will roll itself up into a ball to protect its soft belly. It will also produce a milky fluid that makes its juicy body very unappetizing to predators.

HOW DO TAPEWORMS GET INSIDE PEOPLE?

Humans get tapeworms by eating them. Of course nobody would eat a tapeworm on purpose. Tapeworm larvae, however, hide in the muscles of some cows, pigs, and fish. This means that if people eat the meat of a wormy animal, they're likely to swallow some tapeworms along with their food.

Luckily, people in the United States don't get tapeworms very often. There are several reasons why. In the first place, beef in the United States is inspected for tapeworms before it is sold in the market. Thus, the meat that we buy isn't likely to be wormy. Secondly, even if we eat wormy meat, we won't necessarily become infected. In this country, we usually cook our meat, and tapeworm embryos can't survive a good cooking.

Even under the best of conditions, a newly hatched tapeworm larva has to go on a very hazardous journey that begins when a human swallows a living tapeworm larva. Amazingly, the larva doesn't get digested by powerful chemicals in the stomach and the intestine, like regular food would. The tapeworm's secret is a protective shield made of a thick layer of mucus. This mucus keeps powerful digestive chemicals from killing the tapeworm. In fact, the intestine is such a safe place for the tapeworm, that the unusual creature actually lives there.

Once it has found a home, the tapeworm ensures that it will be able to hang around for a long time. It does this by latching onto the wall of the

host's intestine with its hook-studded head. Then the hungry tapeworm simply soaks up the already digested food that surrounds its body. Because a tapeworm lives off of another living animal, it is considered a *parasite*. Like other parasites, the tapeworm is harmful to its host, because it uses up the host's food.

With all its nutrition readily available, the unpleasant creature has little else to do except grow into an adult and produce eggs. Fully grown tapeworms are often quite long. For example, one particular species, found in raw fish, may reach up to sixty feet in length. Its body will twist and fold so that it can fit neatly into its host's intestine.

The extremely long body of the tapeworm is actually just a string of egg-making sacs. Since a tapeworm has both male and female parts, it can fertilize its own eggs. It may also mate with another tapeworm if one happens to be present. A single animal may have 1,000 sacs, each producing as many as 100,000 eggs. That means 100,000,000 eggs may come out of a single tapeworm!

Eventually, the eggs are released from the sacs and they pass out of the human (or other animal host) with its feces. Next, if wormy human

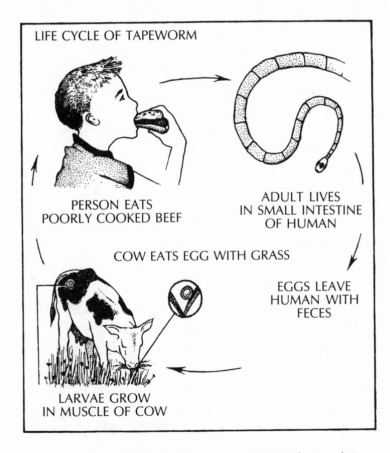

LIFE CYCLE OF TAPEWORM

PERSON EATS
POORLY COOKED BEEF

ADULT LIVES
IN SMALL INTESTINE
OF HUMAN

COW EATS EGG WITH GRASS

EGGS LEAVE
HUMAN WITH
FECES

LARVAE GROW
IN MUSCLE OF COW

feces are deposited in a field where a cow feeds, the cow may eat grass covered with tapeworm eggs. Inside the cow, the eggs hatch, releasing tiny hook-bearing larvae. These larvae pierce through the cow's intestine and make their way into its muscle. Here the patient parasites enclose themselves in a protective sac.

The final stage of the cycle occurs when a human eats the incompletely cooked, larvae-filled beef. As the half-inch-long larvae pass into the human digestive tract, their protective sac dissolves. Out pops a small tapeworm larva which latches onto the human's intestine and begins the cycle all over again.

People who get tapeworms are not necessarily stuck with these nasty creatures for the rest of their lives. Doctors can give their patients special drugs to kill the parasites. Within a few days, the dead tapeworms will pass out of the victim's body during a bowel movement.

WHAT DO LEECHES DO WHEN THEY'RE NOT SUCKING BLOOD?

A leech can put away a six-month supply of blood every time it feeds! This leaves the little vampire with a belly full of blood and lots of extra time. The leech uses its many spare hours to look for mates, produce baby leeches, and just hang around in the water and rest.

The leech's secret to efficient feeding is that it sucks in up to ten times its weight in blood at each meal. Then it squeezes out all the water from the nutritious red liquid. With its water removed, the remaining blood takes up very little space. The leech stores this dried-out food and digests it slowly over a long period of time.

Meanwhile, the well-fed leech can go out and seek a mate. Finding a partner of the right sex is not difficult for these wormlike creatures because every leech is a *hermaphrodite*. This means that it carries both male and female parts in its own body! Despite its remarkable design, a leech does not mate with itself. Instead, it does a double mating with a fellow leech. The male part of each leech mates with the female part of the other. Each partner then produces its own egg-filled cocoon. Some leeches actually attach these sacs to their bodies, protecting the eggs until they hatch.

When its food stores run out, the leech will spend its time in search of the next meal. For water-dwelling species, this means wiggling through the water and seeking out a frog, turtle, fish, human, or other source of blood. For land-living leeches, it means waiting, clinging to a leaf by one sucker, ready to latch onto the first furry mammal that happens along.

CAN AN EARTHWORM LIVE IF IT'S CUT IN HALF?

Many kinds of earthworms are marvelous magicians that can create new heads or tails for themselves almost any time they need to. Our common garden earthworms are not quite as skilled at replacing lost parts, but they can grow back a few segments of a lost tail.

Scientists call the amazing ability to grow new body parts *regeneration*. Of those earthworm species capable of regeneration, the most talented ones do it so well that if they accidentally get cut in half they turn into two worms! As long as there is enough worm left on each cut end, the cut parts can produce whatever is missing, whether it is a new head or a new tail.

It takes a worm only about seven days to replace any lost parts. The newly formed wiggler may grow as large as the parent worm, but never larger.

No one knows exactly how a worm creates a new body for itself. Some scientists believe that changes in the weak electric current that normally runs through the body of an earthworm (or any other animal, for that matter), stimulate new growth in the area around the cut.

The earthworm is not the only creature with the ability to replace its parts. Other lower forms such as sponges, starfish, and flatworms can regenerate from just a piece of the animal's body. In creatures with more complex bodies, however, it becomes harder and harder to recreate lost parts. Many insects and certain vertebrates such as salamanders, lizards, and snakes can regenerate legs or tails. Unfortunately, humans and other mammals aren't particularly good at replacing things. The best that we can do is to regenerate skin, small blood vessels, and liver tissue.

WHY DO EARTHWORMS COME OUT IN THE RAIN?

Earthworms come out in the rain so that they won't drown! Normally, earthworms stay snug and safe in their underground homes. There, they breathe the air that fills the spaces between bits of soil. However, on a rainy day water seeps into the soil spaces, replacing the air that the earthworms need to live. As heavy rains begin to fill the air spaces in the soil, the soggy earthworms crawl to the surface of the ground so that they won't suffocate.

But earthworms don't stay above ground very long. The surface is a dangerous place for these fleshy, delicate creatures. Predators, like birds, can easily snap up juicy earthworms that lie exposed. Furthermore, while too much water is bad for these legless animals, so is too little. In fact, earthworms dry out in the air and eventually die from lack of moisture! Here is the reason why.

Earthworms don't have lungs. Instead, they breathe directly through their skin. An earthworm's skin, like the human lung, needs to be wet in order for oxygen and carbon dioxide to pass through the tissue. Since the outside of the earthworm's skin is unprotected, its wetness evaporates in the dry air. So as soon as the soil dries out a bit, the earthworm returns to its protected underground world where there is just enough moisture to keep it alive.

WHY ARE SLUGS SO SLIMY?

The slimy layer of mucus that covers a slug may seem unpleasant to us, but for the slug it's a real life saver. For one thing, slime provides a smooth, slippery trail for the slug to creep along on. Without this mucous layer, the creature's soft body would be cut and scratched by the bumpy ground. In addition, some slugs also use their slime as a sliding board! After crawling up in tall trees or plants to eat leaves, they release a ribbon of mucus and glide down it to the ground.

Scientists believe that some slugs may also use their slime to mark the location of a safe hiding place. Then they can leave this shelter at night to search for food and simply follow the scent of the slime back home again. This ability is very important to a slug because if the fleshy, shell-less creature is caught without shelter in bright daylight it will soon dry out and die.

Sliminess also helps protect some species of these creepy crawlers from bigger, more aggressive slugs and other predators. For example, when the gray garden slug is bitten, its wound gives off a special milky mucus. This slime apparently tastes nasty because when an attacker gets a mouthful it quickly goes away and tries to wipe off the goo. Other species of slugs use their slime to trick a foe. When an enemy attacks, they release a large puddle of slime and crawl away fast. Confusing the odor of the slime for the slug itself, the attacker may stay at the spot searching for a short while. This gives the intended victim time to escape.

SNAIL AND SLUG

SLIME TRAIL

WHY DO SNAILS HAVE SPIRAL SHELLS?

A snail doesn't have to search to find itself a home. The little animal is always close to shelter, because it carries its house attached to its back. The house is actually a glossy, spiral shell that gives the soft-bodied snail a way to protect itself from predators. When danger threatens, the animal pulls its fleshy head and tail into the coiled spaces of the shell. The hard cover of the spiral shaped house makes it difficult for a predator to get to the tender meat within. As an extra measure of protection, the snail will often squeeze its body and house into a tiny crack or hole where its enemy can't get to it.

Here's where the shell's spiral shape becomes a real bonus. The coiled shape makes the snail's house compact. Although the shell is permanently stuck in its coiled shape, if you could uncoil it, you would find it to be quite long. For example, a shell a half inch long when coiled measures out at four-and-a-half inches uncoiled! Uncoiling the shell would make the snail five times as long as it normally is. If the shell were uncoiled, it would be more difficult for the animal to squeeze into hiding places and also create a rather awkward package for the little creature to carry about. The spiral shape is thus the most compact way to provide living space.

For many snails the shell is more than a well-designed hiding place. To the more than 23,000 land snails, the shell is also a protection against water loss. When the air becomes too dry a snail can slide into its shell and close off the entryway behind it. It does this by covering up the shell's opening with the tough plate, or *operculum*, which attaches to the rear end of its foot. Some snails are able to survive for several years in their closed up house, waiting for the air to become moist enough for them to be able to move about again.

INDEX